Gordy and the Magic Diet

Written by
Kim Diersen & April Runge

Illustrated by
Carrie Hartman

Special Kids Enterprises LP
Chicago, Illinois

To Joshua and Linnea, who taught me that *Magic* diets work! --K.D.

To Nevin and Aiden, may your "*magic*" last forever. -- A.R.

To Stephen G, thanks for all of your "*magical*" advice, wisdom and sushi. --C.H.

Text copyright © 2012 by Special Kids Enterprises LP
Illustration copyright © 2012 by Carrie Hartman

All rights reserved, including the right or reproduction in whole or part in any form without the written permission of the publisher.
ISBN: 978-0-9856460-0-4
Library of Congress Catalog Number: 2012910865

Special Kids Enterprises LP
423 Wiltshire Lane
Crystal Lake, IL 60014

To order, visit www.gordyandthemagicdiet.com

The illustrations in this book were created using india ink, acrylic ink, acrylic paint, pastel and colored pencil on Arches hot press 140lb watercolor paper.
The text type was set in Calibri.
Book design by Carrie Hartman

Printed by Carlith LLC
Carpentersville, IL
September, 2012

Gordy was absolutely, positively certain a Monster lived inside of him.

Not a Hiding-in-the-Closet Monster waiting to cast scary shadows on the wall.

Or an Attack-Your-Teeth-When-You-Forget-to-Brush Monster.

This Monster tiptoed in with a "Shhhh!" that grew slowly through the summer into a big, fat GRRRRR!

Gordy had never felt so bad. "Mom!" Gordy called. "There's a monster inside of me! He makes me feel...

icky, Angry, tired, sick, sad, confused, EXPLOSIVE, ITCHY, STINGING..."

Gordy knew something unusual was happening to him. All through the summer, that Monster kept sneaking up on Gordy.

On the 4th of July, the Monster showed up at Maddie Gerkins' picnic and made Gordy feel ICKY - confused - tired. He had to leave before the fireworks even started.

On August 10th, the Monster showed up at his Cousin Lulu's birthday party and made him feel STINGING - ITCHY - Sad.

Gordy had to leave before it was his turn to hit the piñata.

On September 5th, the Monster showed up at Gordy's School Open House and made him feel

EXPLOSIVE - AngRY - sick.

Gordy had to leave before his parents met his teacher Miss Snodgrass.

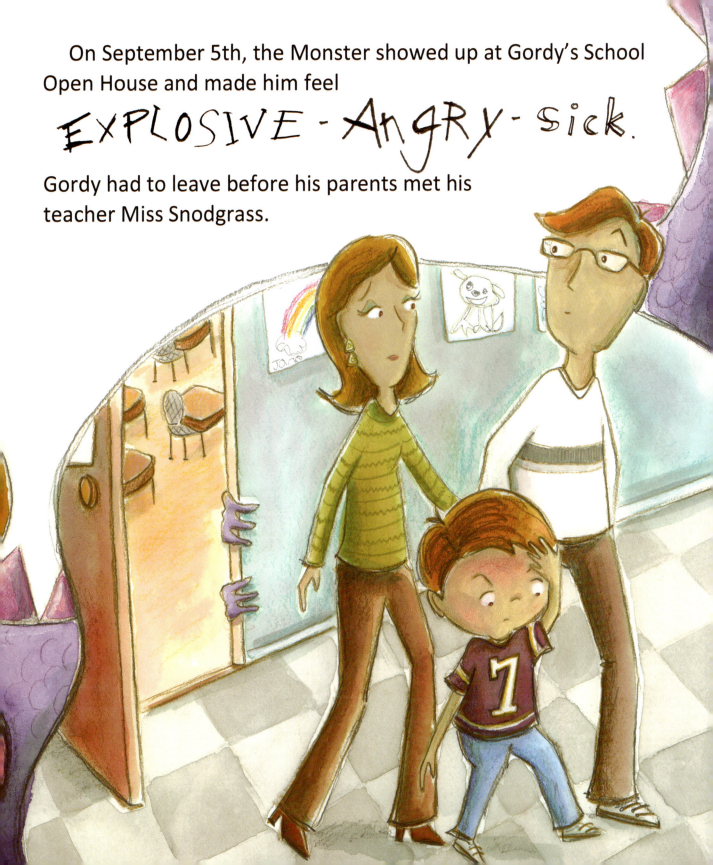

That Monster was taking over Gordy's life. Gordy's Mom was a little concerned, too. So off to the doctor they went. Dr. Bedder looked deep down Gordy's throat. He squeezed, jabbed, poked and prodded Gordy.

"Any Monsters in there?" Gordy asked.

Dr. Bedder shrugged. "Could be," he answered. "But to know for sure we'll need to run a few tests."

"TESTS?" Gordy cried. "I HATE TESTS!" He let out his own monster R-O-O-O-A-R!!!

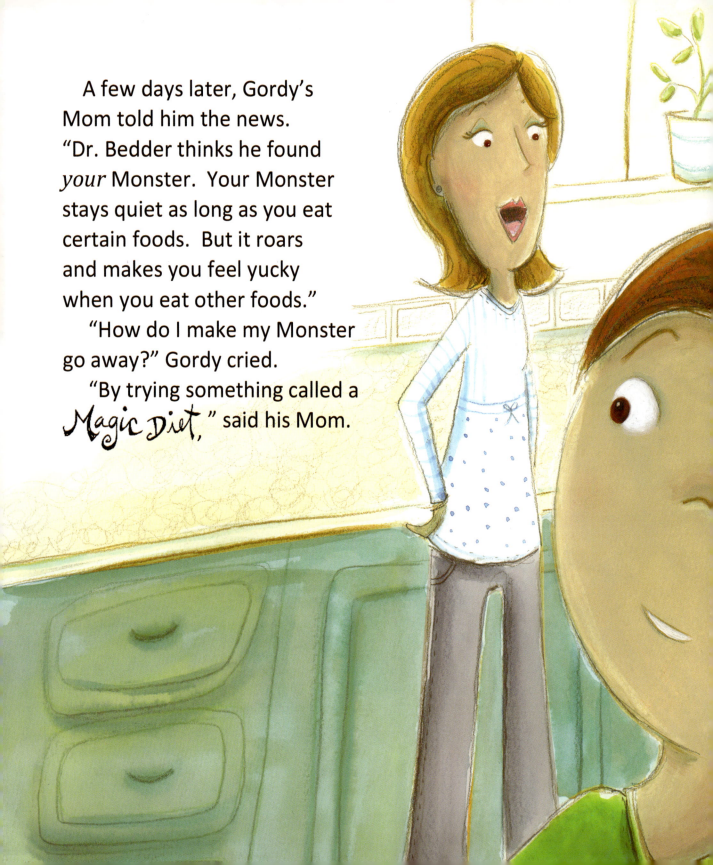

A few days later, Gordy's Mom told him the news. "Dr. Bedder thinks he found *your* Monster. Your Monster stays quiet as long as you eat certain foods. But it roars and makes you feel yucky when you eat other foods."

"How do I make my Monster go away?" Gordy cried.

"By trying something called a *Magic Diet*," said his Mom.

"Will I have to drink a magic potion of green slime from a pond of ooey-gooey sludge?"

Gordy's Mom smiled. "A *Magic Diet* means you eat certain foods and stop eating other foods. We'll know it's working if those yucky Monster feelings disappear."

Gordy liked the idea of no more Monster GRRRRR's!!

The *Magic Diet* began with lunch. Gordy frowned as he sat down in front of his plate. "It smells like dirty socks," he mumbled. It took a *l-o-o-o-o-n-g* time for Gordy to get used to his special diet, but he ate only his *Magic Diet* foods day after day and week after week.

Before Gordy knew it, he forgot about his Monster. Not once had he heard it roar and felt it "GRRRRRR!" "Maybe," Gordy whispered to himself, "my Monster is gone for good!"

There were plenty of times, of course, Gordy wanted to eat foods that weren't a part of his *Magic Diet*. Like lollipops at birthday parties, cotton candy at carnivals and especially cherry slushies on hot, fall days.

It was hard saying "No, thank you!" all the time but Gordy stayed strong. That is, until it was time to visit Grandma, his Grandma who baked **The World's Best Double-Fudge Chocolate Cake with sprinkles on top.** Gordy could smell the cake from half-way down the street.

While Gordy's Mom explained his *Magic Diet* to Grandma, Gordy snuck into the kitchen to admire Grandma's cake.

"Maybe a teeny-tiny piece won't hurt," Gordy thought. After all, the Monster hadn't roared once since he'd begun his *Magic Diet*.

In no time at all, Gordy heard the "GRRRRR!"
"Go away, Monster!" Gordy moaned. "No more cake for me!" But it was too late. All the yucky monster feelings were back. Gordy curled up and cried himself to sleep on Grandma's lap.

The months flew by and Gordy started feeling a little nervous. There were only three more days until Halloween. It was his favorite holiday and candy was NOT on his *Magic Diet* list.

Gordy quickly got to work on his costume and after he finished, he held up his sword of strength and made a promise to himself.

"I will fight my Monster! I will keep him quiet! I am Gordy the Pirate on a *Magic Diet*!"

That night, Gordy ran from house to house, filling his Trick-or-Treat bag to the very top. When two Choc-o-logs spilled out, Gordy's mouth watered.

"What if I took just one teeny-tiny bite? Would one little square wake up the Monster?"

Gordy didn't have to think too long before he remembered the last time he'd heard his Monster roar, when he'd only eaten a fingerful of Grandma's Double-Fudge Chocolate Cake.

He put the two Choc-o-logs back inside his bag, waved his sword of strength and headed home.

When Gordy returned home, he dumped his bag full of candy onto the kitchen table.

"Here, Mom," Gordy said, pushing the mountain of candy toward her. "You can have my candy. I found the real pirate treasure."

"What's that?" asked his Mom.

"No more GRRRRRs!" Gordy exclaimed.

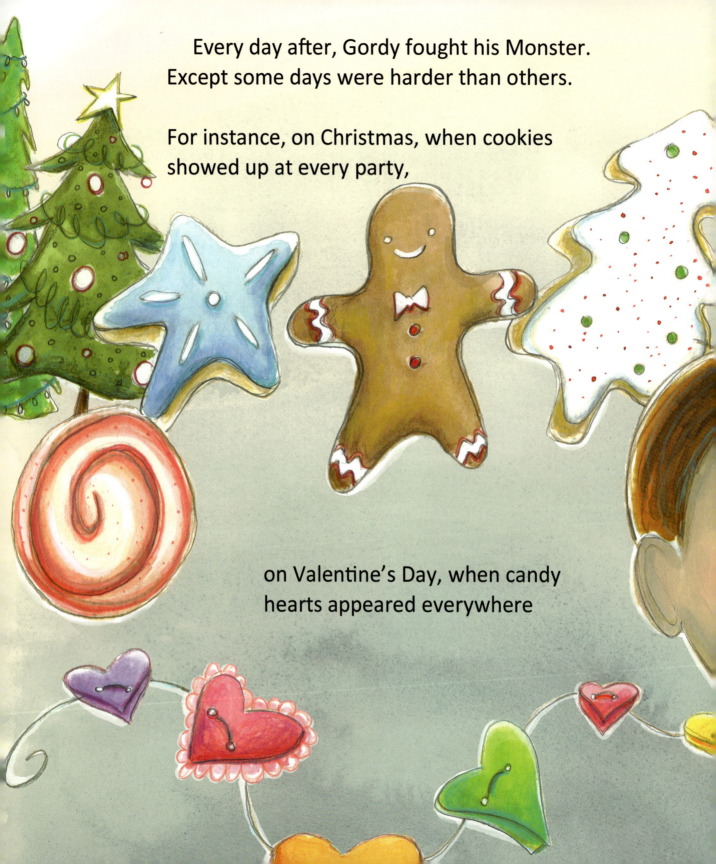

Every day after, Gordy fought his Monster. Except some days were harder than others.

For instance, on Christmas, when cookies showed up at every party,

on Valentine's Day, when candy hearts appeared everywhere

and on Easter, when every Easter basket, *except his,* held chocolate bunnies.

Still, Gordy was absolutely, positively certain that his Monster would stay quiet now... thanks to his *Magic Diet.*

When a Monster moves in, the joy of life moves out! We discovered early-on that our son had a Monster that was causing all kinds of yucky "symptoms". When he strictly adhered to his "Magic Diet"--a gluten-free, artificial-free diet--his tantrums were reduced, he had more emotional stability and he began to enjoy and engage with the world around him. He has been on his "Magic Diet" for 6 years now, and every time he gives in to that "Chocolate Cake Temptation", the monster shows up with a Grrrrrrr! Living on a "Magic Diet" is a journey that has its challenges, but it is so worth it!
- *Kim Diersen*

The Monster in our home was a beastly sort, more like an invisible terrorist. Our daughter was diagnosed with catastrophic pediatric epilepsy for which there was no known cause, but a very poor prognosis. The doctors tried to tame the hundreds of daily seizures through various cocktails of anti-epilepsy medications that left her a zombie and shell of a child. After starting the highly restrictive Ketogenic Diet, our daughter quickly emerged from the medication fog. Within 4 months, the hundreds of seizures disappeared and over time, medications were weaned. She now lives life as a healthy seizure-free and medication-free child. This special medical diet was a very magical gift.
- *April Runge*

We discovered a few Monsters of our own lurking about our home. Gluten tends to make my oldest daughter's tummy ROAR loudly. My other daughter's Monster is preservatives. By discovering our family's intolerance to processing these ingredients, we have been able to greatly reduce the headaches, achiness, tiredness, mood swings and tummy aches that were daily occurrences. Bye-bye, Monster!
- *Carrie Hartman*